The Literary Detective

A Guide to the Study of Great Literary Works

2nd Edition

by Glen Paul Hammond

Cover Illustration by G.P.H

Table of Contents

Introduction

You are deciding on your next book to read. You enter your local bookstore and notice the current bestsellers lined up neatly in front of you. You recognize some of the titles from comments you have heard at work or on the radio. The bookstore has them situated near the entrance and turned so that their front covers face the doorway. You remember seeing many of the same books at your local drugstore. You move forward, leaving the current day's bestseller list behind. Rows and rows of books slide past you. You stop and pick up a small black and red paperback. It is John Steinbeck's *Of Mice and Men.* You study the cover and ask yourself this question: "How is a great literary work like *Of Mice and Men* different from a bestseller you commonly find at a drugstore?"

This is a question often asked by individuals who are about to begin reading a work from what Harold Bloom calls "the canon." After all, why should you read a book that is as challenging to read as it is entertaining? Why not just read a work of pure entertainment? The answer to these questions establishes not only the reason why a reader should study the great works, but also illustrates the way in which such works must be approached.

The Nobel Prize winning author Ernest Hemingway suggested in his *Theory of Omission* that great writing was like an iceberg: most of the knowledge is contained in the underwater part of the iceberg (fig. 1). This largest part of the iceberg is unseen. A book meant purely to entertain, on the other hand, is like a buoy floating on top of the water: most of the knowledge is contained in the part seen by the reader, what the author has actually written on the page (fig. 2). In a work of great literature, the visible part of the iceberg corresponds to the surface plot of the work, which can be found on the back cover of the book. This part is good for a book report. A great literary essay, however, always deals with the unseen part, which contains the greater knowledge or underlying meaning of the work. This is really what the writer wants you to understand. It is this part of the work that transports you into the pages so that the book's deeper message becomes meaningful to you.

Approaching great literature in this way provides the reader with a new perspective that serves to illuminate the many layers that make up the entirety of the work. Such a full understanding of Mark Twain's **The Adventures of Huckleberry Finn**, for example, reveals the deeper meanings embedded in the text and, as a result, allows the reader to achieve a core understanding of the work.

In a diagrammatical iceberg, Twain's great literary masterpiece can be viewed in the following way:

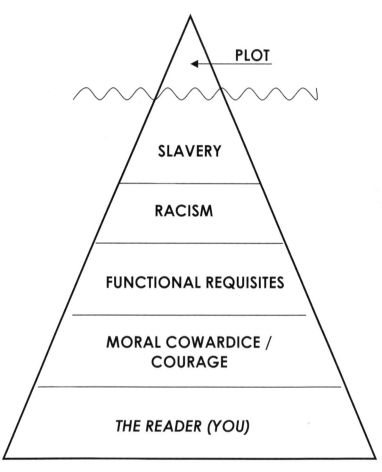

Above the waterline is the plot. In the case of **The Adventures of Huckleberry Finn**, this can be summed up as involving a runaway white boy and slave, who travel down the Mississippi River together; it is simplistic and mundane. Moving just a little deeper below the surface, however, is a common and acknowledged understanding of the basic theme of the novel, the great American sin of slavery.

The theme of slavery is based in the historical time period or setting of the novel, which is pre-civil war United States. In order to achieve the best position to understand the work, the reader must research the time period and culture being represented. This will inevitably lead to an investigation of the culture's deeply rooted racism.

At this point, the reader begins to understand that by exploring the historical time period presented in the novel, the reader is able to free the novel from the constraints of a strictly historical perspective. Essentially, by placing the novel in its historical time, the reader can bring it out of that time period and into the present. The fact that the novel itself was written well after the end of slavery, suggests that the institution of slavery was not the essential matter that Twain was exploring.

Indeed, racism as a fatal characteristic of human nature, which transcends time and place, can now be viewed as a deeper underlying theme. Even though many discussions of the novel will delve no deeper than this important layer, it is evident from the very first chapter that Twain's book means to go much further in its exploration on how societies operate. Through repetition, the author introduces the existence of what social scientists now call *functional requisites*, which are basic functions that each member of society must observe if the society is to function in a particular way. For a slave state society to accept the institutional law of slavery, racism had to become a basic function.

Colonel Sherburn's famous speech in chapter 22 and a cross reference to how it reflects Twain's own view on "man's commonest weakness, his aversion to being unpleasantly conspicuous," introduces the even deeper theme of moral courage. Once the individual recognizes that society requires them to observe certain basic functions, the individual is made cognizant of issues that involve the morality of accepting immoral societal norms. As Twain remarks, only one individual in 10,000 is capable of the courage to stand alone against the larger group and, in the novel, *that* individual is the delinquent Huckleberry Finn.

Since functional requisites, moral cowardice/courage and the dilemmas they represent are things that all individuals potentially face in various ways and in various degrees on a daily basis, the book is now completely relevant to the reader's immediate life, and the deepest layer of any read has been accomplished: You!

When a piece of literature tells you something about yourself, not only does the work seem to come alive, but it also allows the reader to apply what has been learned to their everyday life. The most ancient of texts suddenly becomes intimate and applicable to the modern reader.

It is at this point that the individual comes to understand the true value of great literary works. They contain the seeds of wisdom.

In order for this to occur, however, the reader must learn how to access that wisdom; the reader must learn how to get at that unseen part of the iceberg.

It is this process that turns a mediocre reader into a literary detective.

Glen Paul Hammond
July 2014

Fig. 1 The Nobel Prize winning author Ernest Hemingway suggested in his *Theory of Omission* that great writing was like an iceberg; most of the knowledge is contained in the underwater part of the iceberg.

Fig. 2 A book meant purely to entertain is like a buoy floating on the surface of the water: most of the knowledge is contained in the part seen by the reader, what the author has actually written on the page.

Sleuthing

A literary detective is a reader whose duty is to detect, through in-depth investigation, underlying meanings in literary texts. Literary detectives seek all the facts in attempting to discover what the author is actually trying to communicate. They gather, organize, and creatively use information.

The Creative Relationship

In the creative relationship between writer and reader, the writer provides the reader with clues that the reader must piece together. In this relationship, the reader will treat these clues as puzzle pieces. Once these pieces are put together to form a picture, the reader will have to make an educated guess as to what the picture is trying to convey. This is the process of investigation for the literary detective. The gathering of clues is the preliminary investigation and the deduction of clues is the final investigation.

Characteristics of Five Classic Detectives

"How often have I said to you that when you have eliminated the impossible, whatever remains, however improbable, must be the truth?"

Sherlock Holmes

Confidence, Logic, and Astute Observation:

When Mr. Holmes speaks, he speaks with the authority of someone who expects people to listen. His expert use of deduction follows the practice of amassing a large body of evidence. This evidence is creatively and logically used to produce a number of possible explanations. These explanations are then narrowed down to the one that best accounts for the collected evidence.

Modus Operandi:

The good literary detective must employ the persistent research skills of a Sherlock Holmes when seeking out the author's clues. Applying logic and deduction to these clues, the literary detective must then find the best possible explanation and assert its validity with confidence.

"If I wasn't hard, I wouldn't be alive. If I wasn't gentle, I wouldn't deserve to be alive."

Philip Marlowe

Involvement, Enjoyment, and Sensitivity:

Whether it is being beaten, drugged, arrested, seduced, or insulted, this detective fully participates in the lives and dramas of his clients. His love of chess explains the enjoyment he has in working out the problems that his profession presents him. He chases after clues with hardboiled persistence, but also looks at things in a more sensitive and human way: not every deduction is simply an interpretation of the cold, hard facts.

Modus Operandi:

The literary detective gets involved in the work by putting his or her own life experience into the interpretation of the author's themes. This fulfills the detective's part of the creative relationship between writer and reader. It is this effort that makes the work meaningful to the individual reader. The literary detective enjoys the quest to discover a work's truth the way a chess player enjoys the challenge of the next move. Even though it may seem difficult or impossible at times, the literary detective enjoys the process of exploration as much as the discovery. Finally, a good literary detective must be able to step outside the box of cold, hard fact and interpret clues with a sensitive eye.

"Intuition is like reading a word without having to spell it out."
Miss Jane Marple

Passion, Patterns, and Work:

With a passion that borders on ruthlessness, Miss Marple pursues the truth and never gives up. Famous for her use of patterns, this detective evaluates new situations by finding comparisons from figures and events in her own past. For example, one of her clients clarifies, "If a thing reminds you of something else…it's probably the same kind of thing." Once she finds a plausible pattern, she works and works at the details until it leads her to the deductive truth.

Modus Operandi:

The literary detective must never give up. The search for literary clues is a kind of treasure hunt, and only those who persevere discover the prize. The literary detective must be sensitive to patterns created by the author. He or she must also be knowledgeable about patterns in both the author's as well as the reader's own literary and real past. This will often help in deciphering present clues. Though at first the literary detective's investigation may seem far-fetched or (as is often the case with Miss Marple) confused, with intuitive hard work all can be brought into focus.

"It is the brain, the little gray cells on which one must rely."
Hercule Poirot

Psychology and Gray Cells:

Using human behaviour to understand humans is a skill that this detective has perfected. By attending to the psychology of the case, Hercule Poirot is able to recreate the case's events. His observations gain lucidity through the tremendous exercise of brain power. Focusing his gray cells on the known events leads this detective to discover evidence that is, as yet, unknown. "One should not ask for outside proof," he is quoted as saying once. "No, reason should be enough."

Modus Operandi:

Understanding his or her own self and motivations will help the literary detective understand character behaviours and the motivations behind them. In the end, there is no substitute for quiet and concentrated thinking. Ultimately, in the reading of a work meant to personally inform the reader, it is only the reader that can be relied upon.

"It will be found, in fact, that the ingenious are always fanciful, and the truly imaginative never otherwise than analytic."
C. Auguste Dupin

Mathematician and Poet:

This detective combines the objectivity of a mathematician with the intuition and creativity of a poet. He is a man of two minds: an objective observer who remains necessarily detached, as well as an individual who seeks to identify with the crime's perpetrator by taking on the criminal's viewpoint.

Modus Operandi:

The literary detective must remain both detached and intimately involved in the work being investigated. The literary detective must be able to objectively observe the author's characters while at the same time taking on their perspectives to fully understand them. In a way similar to that of Philip Marlowe participating in the lives and dramas of his clients, this very intimate involvement sustains the creative relationship between author and reader. If this relationship is severed, textual understanding is lost.

Exercise at the Lab

1. Which of the above detectives is the most similar to you? In what ways?

2. Which detective would you like to resemble more? Why?

3. Do you have another favourite detective not listed above? If so,

create a *Profile* and *Modus Operandi* for that detective.

4. Create a *Profile* and *Modus Operandi* that best describes the kind of detective you think you would be.

Tools of the Trade

Just as Sherlock Holmes had his magnifying glass or Hercule Poirot his dispatch case and forceps, the successful literary detective is in need of certain tools of the trade.

Pen/Pencil:
It is important to mark potential clues for later study.

Dictionary:
Since words are the medium that the writer uses to communicate, understanding the many applications and meaning of a word is essential.

Author Biography:
Even a short blurb can aid the reader in putting the investigated work into proper context.

Historical Context:
A work's place in history helps to define it and therefore helps the investigator to understand it. A study of the historical period being described in the work and the historical period at the time of the work's publication is important.

Sticky notes:
Keeping track of collected clues in an organized way will help in the final investigation.

Notebook:
Write down immediate reactions to potential clues in a notebook or in the book's margins.

Critical Analysis:
Peruse what literary critics have said about the text.

Study Place:
Find a place that is conducive to concentrated reading.

Study Partners:
Ask an informed friend for opinions.

Study Notes:
For most great works, there are simplified and informative notes that can be purchased.

Library and Internet:
Both of these tools are useful for additional information.

Exercise at the Lab

1. Which of the above tools are you missing?

2. How will you acquire those missing tools?

3. What tools not listed above do you think would be helpful? Why?

Villains

Every detective, regardless of stature, must deal with villains both great and small. Below is a list of villains that, if given the chance, will impede any investigation.

Lack of Confidence:
The literary detective must be confident enough to both collect and creatively interpret clues. Lack of confidence is often resolved by experience and practice.

Timidity:
The detective must be bold in investigating clues and associating them with facts.

Impatience:
Literary detection is meticulous, time-consuming work and the investigator must have the patience to search and sift out all valid clues.

Laziness:
The one clue quickly skimmed over could be the very clue that leads to a breakthrough.

Distraction:
Every detective must at some point employ deep and uninterrupted contemplation. Distraction (in all its varied forms) must be either eliminated or kept to a minimum.

Disorganization:
Great detectives do not allow their own disorganization to further complicate the already difficult task of investigation. Since the key to success is often the collection and organization of sometimes confusing pieces of evidence, an organized workplace is essential.

Intimidaion:

This is perhaps the archenemy of the literary detective. The investigator must always remember that literature is created by individuals who simply wish to communicate their ideas to readers. Whereas someone you know may communicate with you over a coffee at a café or restaurant, the author is simply performing the same act through written words.

Exercise at the Lab

1. From the above, list your top three villains:

        A._____
        B._____
        C._____

2. What other villains, not listed above, may impede your investigative abilities?

        A._____
        B._____
        C._____

3. What steps can you take to rid yourself of these villains?

Method

"All good detective work is a mere matter of method."
Hercule Poirot

Becoming a good reader is essentially the method involved in becoming a good detective of literature. Just as a detective is trained to find clues at a crime scene, so too can the reader be trained to detect clues left by the author. One good example is repetition. In John Steinbeck's classic novel ***Of Mice and Men***, the author repeats a certain idea like the importance of friendship again and again. With this use of repetition, the author is, in effect, leaning over the reader's shoulder and emphatically pointing these passages out as essential. An awareness of this can precipitate an investigation that involves comparing an idea in Chapter Seven with an idea in Chapter One. This is what is known as critical thinking.

Simple methods of detection incorporated into the act of reading differentiate the good reader from the bad, the mediocre literary detective from the good. Regarding the simplicity of method, the famous detective Hercule Poirot asserted in ***The Mysterious Affair At Styles***:

> *One fact leads to another – so we continue. Does the next fit in with that? A merveille! Good! We can proceed. This next little fact – no! Ah, that is curious! There is something missing – a link in the chain that is not there. We examine. We search. And that little curious fact, that possible paltry little detail that will not tally, we put it here!*

Included in the methodology of clues to be discussed are forms of *repetition, title, quotations, genre, associative pairing, key words,* and *page space.*

The Title

"'Rache' is the German for 'revenge;' so don't lose your time looking for Miss Rachel."
Sherlock Holmes, regarding a one-word message left by a murder victim, *A Study In Scarlet*

Much like a victim's final message left at a crime scene, the title of a work is always a good place to start an investigation. In fact, it is one of the most direct ways for a writer to grab a reader's attention. Since even the smallest actions of a writer are directed toward some definite and practical end, something as large and important as a *Title* demands its fair share of a literary detective's attention.

In **Old Man at the Bridge,** by Ernest Hemingway, the title establishes the *Old Man* as the subject of the story. Immediately the reader knows where to focus attention in order to properly interpret the story's deeper meaning.

The *Bridge* is another focal point in both the title and therefore the story. The *Bridge* is the only escape route for evacuees under attack during the Spanish Civil War. As the title confirms, the story is about an *Old Man* and his inability to escape during time of war. He is unable to cross the *Bridge* to safety. The *Old Man* is literally stuck at the *Bridge*. Hemingway is showing the reader what many history books never mention: the plight of a helpless individual during time of war. Since the *Old Man* is unable to cross the *Bridge*, he is unable to save his own life and, as a consequence, will become a nameless victim of the Spanish conflict.

In Katherine Mansfield's short-story **Bliss,** the reader can cross reference a study of the story's main character with a hypothesis about the title. The main character is a woman living in England in the early part of the last century. Due to oppression against women, common at the time, she is unable to change her life circumstances and is, as a result, invested in remaining unaware of them. In this way, the title of **Bliss** can be understood to mean *Ignorance is Bliss.*

The Great Gatsby by F. Scott Fitzgerald is another fine example. The reader understands immediately who the protagonist is (in this case Jay Gatsby) and that there is something special about him: he is great!

Exercise at the Crime Scene

The Red Badge of Courage is an anti-war novel by Stephan Crane. The work depicts the experiences of a young soldier during the American Civil War. By showing what combat is really like, the novel aims to dispel romantic illusions about war.

1. How might the title act as a clue to this underlying theme?

2. What might the word *red* signify?

Note: It is important to remember that once the detective has discovered a clue, he or she must make an educated guess about its possible meaning.

Introduction of Characters

"Let him, on meeting a fellow-mortal, learn at a glance to distinguish the history of the man, and the trade or profession to which he belongs... Observation with me is second nature."
Sherlock Holmes, A Study in Scarlett

Most often, the function of Chapter One in the modern novel is to introduce the characters. Once the author has introduced the characters, he or she can get on with the telling of the story. A good writer uses every part of the novel to aid the reader in understanding the underlying meaning of the work. For this, an understanding of the characters is essential. The literary detective must be able to detect all the devices and subtle clues that are being offered.

In its introduction of main characters, ***The Great Gatsby*** is a fine example of both *device* and *essential characteristics* at work.

Essential Characteristics:

Being aware of the author's choice of words, such as the kinds of adjectives and adverbs surrounding a character, is one of the easiest ways to discover what the author intends us to understand about a particular individual. Just as the great detective Sherlock Holmes encouraged sharpening the faculties of observation, in order to teach one where to look and what to look for, the good literary detective will observe key words that will immediately help to distinguish a character.

In the case of Tom Buchanan, negative words like *arrogant* and *cruel* inundate both initial and later appearances of the character:

> *Now he was a sturdy straw-haired man of thirty with a rather **hard** mouth and a **supercilious** manner. Two shining **arrogant** eyes had established dominance over his face and gave him the appearance of always leaning **aggressively** forward. Not even the effeminate swank of his riding clothes could hide the **enormous** power of that body...It was a body capable of **enormous***

*leverage – a **cruel** body.*

The key words in bold are subtly presented in the author's description of the character and his movements, but the intended effect is unmistakable. This is best appreciated by separating the key words from the context of Fitzgerald's descriptive paragraph: *hard, supercilious, arrogant, aggressively, enormous,* and *cruel.* Consequently, the reader's first impression of Mr. Buchanan is a negative one. This is not a person anyone should be interested in meeting.

On the other hand, notice the adjectives and nouns used to describe Jay Gatsby in the same chapter:

> *If personality is an unbroken series of successful gestures, then there was something **gorgeous** about him, some **heightened sensitivity** to the promises of life, as if he were related to one of those intricate machines that register earthquakes ten thousand miles away. This **responsiveness**…was an extraordinary **gift** for **hope**, a **romantic** readiness such as I have never found in any other person and which it is not likely I shall ever find again.*

Through the use of adjectives and nouns alone (*gorgeous, heightened, sensitivity, responsiveness, gift, hope, romantic*), Fitzgerald introduces Jay Gatsby as Tom Buchanan's complete opposite. This foreshadows the future adversarial relationship between the two, which takes on symbolic significance as the novel develops. Furthermore, in the battle between Tom Buchanan and Jay Gatsby, the author establishes early the side he wishes the reader to be on – namely, Jay Gatsby's.

Device:

Writers will use different devices to certain effect. As with motive in a criminal investigation, understanding the intent of the effect by recognizing the device is an entry point into understanding the text.

In *The Great Gatsby*, F. Scott Fitzgerald creates curiosity about Jay Gatsby by making him mysterious. He does this in at least eight ways.

1. The title of the book, *The Great Gatsby,* is named after Jay Gatsby. This is especially relevant as it is pointed out by the novel's narrator in the first chapter: "Only Gatsby, the man who gives his name to this book…"
2. The title distinguishes the character as *Great*.
3. The key words used to describe him (see above) make Jay Gatsby seem awe-inspiring.
4. The narrator singles him out as the only individual exempt from blame: "Only Gatsby…was exempt from my reaction."
5. Gatsby is described as prey, foreshadowing his tragedy.
6. In a very normal way, we meet every other character in the book. Yet, until Chapter Three, we only hear about Gatsby and see him acting mysteriously from afar – he appears and disappears like a ghost.
7. Gatsby's name is mentioned at the Buchanan household; Daisy reacts strangely to it and then is interrupted so that we are left curious as to the reasons for her unorthodox behaviour.
8. The narrator tells us Gatsby is unique and that he is not likely ever to meet such a man again.

In effect, then, the rest of the characters are introduced to the reader as nonchalantly as anyone would be introduced to strangers at a party. At the same time –and to continue the party metaphor – for the entire evening the reader is baited with talk of a Jay Gatsby. The reader is incredibly curious and waiting for Gatsby to arrive, watching the door in hopes of seeing him walk in.

John Steinbeck's *Of Mice and Men* uses a similar device to distinguish Slim, the prime example of good in the novel, from the rest of the characters introduced.

All the other characters are introduced to the reader with their dress and actions being the main descriptive element. For example, in Chapter Two the Boss appears:

A little stocky man stood in the open doorway. He wore blue jean trousers, a flannel shirt, a black, unbuttoned vest and a black coat. His thumbs were stuck in his belt, on each side of a square steel buckle. On his head was a soiled brown Stetson hat, and he wore high-heeled boots and spurs to prove he was not a laboring man.

On the other hand, Slim's first appearance in the same chapter is the only one in which an individual's character traits (rather than dress and mundane actions) are described:

*A tall man stood in the doorway. He held a crushed Stetson hat under his arm while he combed his long, black, damp hair straight back. Like the others he wore blue jeans and a short denim jacket. When he had finished combing his hair he moved into the room, and he moved with a **majesty** only achieved by **royalty** and **master** craftsmen. He was a jerkline skinner, the **prince** of the ranch, capable of driving ten, sixteen, even twenty mules with a single line to the leaders. He was capable of killing a fly on the wheeler's butt with a bull whip without touching the mule. There was a **gravity** in his manner and a **quiet** so **profound** that all talk stopped when he spoke. His **authority** was so great that his word was taken on any subject, be it politics or **love**. This was Slim, the jerkline skinner. His hatchet face was **ageless.** He might have been thirty-five or fifty. His ear heard more than was said to him, and his slow speech had overtones not of thought, but of **understanding** beyond thought. His hands, large and lean, were as **delicate** in their action as those of a **temple dancer.***

Note the key words in bold and note also that the paragraph begins the same way as the one describing Boss, but then shifts away from Slim's clothes to his glowing character. Slim, unlike everyone else in the book, is more than his clothes or outward appearance – he is a man whose character demands recognition.

Exercise at the Crime Scene

Essential Characteristics:

A detective is trained to notice characteristics of an individual that would escape a less observant person. Based on first impressions and using essential characteristics, observe the following character from Virginia Woolfe's novel *Mrs. Dalloway*:

> *...She saw him [Septimus Smith] sitting in his shabby overcoat alone, on the seat, hunched up, staring.*

As a literary detective, you must remember to use your principal clues. In this case, the principal clues are the key words: *shabby, alone, hunched,* and *staring.* Also note that these physical descriptors are meant to be representative of the character's mental state.

1. Based on first impressions and using essential characteristics, what observations would you make about the above character?

2. Replace the key words in the following paragraph (a) with their opposites or antonyms in paragraph (b):

    a) "If personality is an unbroken series of successful gestures, then there was something **gorgeous** about him, some heightened **sensitivity** to the promises of life, as if he were related to one of those intricate machines that register earthquakes ten thousand miles away. This responsiveness...was an extraordinary **gift** for hope, a **romantic** readiness such as I have never found in any other person and which it is not likely I shall ever find again.

b) "If personality is an unbroken series of successful gestures, then there was something _ugly_ about him, some heightened _sold_ to the promises of life, as if he were related to one of those intricate machines that register earthquakes ten thousand miles away. This responsiveness…was an extraordinary _____ for _____, a _____ readiness such as I have never found in any other person and which it is not likely I shall ever find again.

3. How did the use of antonyms affect your understanding of the character?

Device:

Notice the introductory entrance of John Steinbeck's two main characters, George and Lennie, in the first chapter of his novel *Of Mice and Men*:

> *They had walked in single file down the path, and even in the open one stayed behind the other.*

1. What important clue to the relationship between these two characters is being given here?

Establishing Genre

"The measures, then…were good in their kind, and well executed;
their defect lay in their being inapplicable to the case… He [the
Prefect] perpetually errs by being too deep or too shallow for the
matter in hand."

C. Auguste Dupin, ***The Purloined Letter***

Genre is a category of literature characterized by a certain form,
style, or subject matter. Establishing the genre of a work is
important, because it helps us look in the right places for the writer's
clues. As C. Auguste Dupin asserted, the literary detective must
learn to adapt the method of investigation to the particular demands
of the case at hand. Since, for example, we know John Steinbeck's
Of Mice and Men is an allegory, we immediately understand the
importance of the characters as representative types. We understand
that in this particular genre we do not need to investigate too deeply
into the individual personalities of each character. In an allegory, the
author teaches an abstract truth or moral principle – basically, the
difference between right and wrong or good and evil. The story's
fictional characters teach the moral lessons. The author will not
construct complex real-life characters, but rather invent simple
representative types that will be all good or all bad or very simply in-
between. This is because the author does not want the characters to
get in the way of the life lessons being taught.

In Steinbeck's ***Of Mice and Men***, the life lessons teach the reader
how to be a good person. Boss's black vest and boots, Curly's
aggressive behaviour and gloved hand filled with Vaseline place
them, upon first meeting, in the bad category, while characters more
neutrally dressed are initially placed in the in-between category.
Slim, distinguished as he is by his introductory paragraph (see page
27), on the other hand, is solidly understood to be alone in the good
category. In Steinbeck's allegory, Slim is the prime example of what
we should aspire toward.

Another example in the importance of establishing genre is
George Orwell's satire ***Animal Farm***. A satire is a written

composition that criticizes some vice or folly through ridicule and contempt. Humour is used to teach a serious lesson: to point out some problem or evil in the real world. Since we know it is a satire, we know that the characters involved are comical renditions of serious examples in real life. In Orwell's **Animal Farm**, the political view being satirized is communism. However, the reasons as to why movements such as communism must fail are also being pointed at in the novel. Consequently, Orwell also satirizes the human propensity for power and greed.

The satirical characters in Orwell's novel are understood to represent different facets of society. For example, the sheep represent the uneducated masses that are easily controlled by propaganda and slogans. The sheep need to be controlled so the pigs can establish power; the pigs wish to establish power in order to satisfy their greed. This exposes a very human problem that exists in the real world. George Orwell makes sure that the reader understands greed is a human problem by transforming the pigs into humans at the novel's end.

Exercise at the Crime Scene

Becoming familiar with the different categories of literature is important in determining genre.

1. How many different categories of literature do you know?

       A. _____
       B. _____
       C. _____
       D. _____
       E. _____
       F. _____

Repetition

"Tiptoes! tiptoes! Square, too, quite unusual boots! They come, they go, they come again…"
Sherlock Holmes, The Boscombe Valley Mystery

Words:

Repetition of *words* is one of the author's most noticeable and easily identified clues. Talented writers suffer from no shortage of words or alternatives that mean the same thing. By choosing to use the same word repeatedly, the writer wishes to draw attention to it.

In **The Great Gatsby**, F. Scott Fitzgerald uses the word "*change*" as well as secondary words with a similar meaning to imply the unreliability of the people who attend Gatsby's parties. Since they are always changing, they cannot be counted on or trusted:

> *The groups **change** more swiftly, **swell** with new arrivals, **dissolve** and **form** in the same breath; already there are wanderers, confident girls who weave **here and there** among the stouter and more stable, become for a sharp, joyous moment the center of a group, and then, excited with triumph, glide on through the sea-**change** of faces and voices and color under the constantly **changing** light.*

Arthur Miller uses repetition to highlight the problem of dream versus reality in his play **Death of a Salesman.** He does this by having one of his characters repeat the word "fact."

> *BIFF: All day, as a matter of cold **fact**. And a lot of – instances – **facts**, Pop, **facts** about my life came back to me… Let's hold on to the **facts** tonight, Pop.*

In Ernest Hemingway's short story **A Clean Well-Lighted Place**, the dirty dark of the grave and the meaninglessness or nothingness attached to a life doomed to end in death are underlined by the author repeating the word *nothing* in two languages:

> *It was a **nothing** that he knew too well. It was all a **nothing** and a man was **nothing** too. It was only that and light was all it needed and a certain cleanness and order. Some lived in it and never felt it but he knew it all was **nada** y pues **nada** y **nada** y pues **nada**…*

Scenes:

Repetition of scenes is also an indication of a potential clue to be found. Whenever a writer goes back to the same locale and allows for descriptive comparisons, the intent is to remind the reader of the previous scene. Juxtaposing or putting the two scenes side by side often leads to an insight into the text.

In ***The Great Gatsby***, readers who visited the Buchanan household in Chapter One return there in Chapter Seven. When the two scenes are placed side by side, there are many descriptive similarities. These similarities serve to highlight the one constant glaring addition to the latter scene. Whereas Tom, Nick, Jordan, and Daisy were present in Chapter One, now Jay Gatsby is present and has entered the life of Tom's wife, Daisy Buchanan (see *Table 1*)

Since there are so many similarities between Chapter One (when Daisy had not been reunited with Gatsby) and Chapter Seven (when she is in the midst of a serious affair with him), the reader understands something that Gatsby does not: Gatsby has had very little to no impact on Daisy's life and, contrary to what she tells him, she is not planning to make him part of any significant life change. He is a non-factor in the lives of Daisy and Tom Buchanan. The introduction of Daisy's daughter is another difference in the two chapters that further highlights the impossibility of Gatsby's dream for a new life with Daisy.

George Orwell also uses scene repetition in his novel ***Animal Farm.*** The author has the animals return to the same knoll the reader encountered six chapters earlier. In Chapter One, after the animals' rebellion has been successfully achieved and their human oppressors vanquished, the animals celebrate at a knoll. Then in Chapter Seven, following public executions perpetrated by their former comrades, the pigs, the animals return to the same knoll. Scene repetition reminds the reader of the incidents that started the animals dreaming of their own farm in the first place, a farm where they could live without fear and in freedom (see *Table 2*)

The similarities between the two scenes serve to highlight the contrast – George Orwell points to the failure of the original dream of Animal Farm by allowing the reader to compare the dream in Chapter One with the reality in Chapter Seven. The reality illustrated in the later chapter falls far short of the idealistic vision outlined in the earlier one. The reader now understands that the dream is dead.

An understanding of genre along with scene repetition helps the literary detective visualize what is read in Arthur Miller's play ***Death of a Salesman***. This understanding serves to elucidate the author's intent when repeating scenes at the beginning of Acts I and II. Since it is a play, the reader should visualize what would physically be presented on a stage. In the beginning of these two acts, the audience sees two older people sitting alone in their kitchen. The scene of two older people sitting alone and discussing their past is a doleful one. They discuss the hopes and dreams they had when first married as well as the nature of life and death. The audience and, therefore, the reader witness the sad scene of two older people discussing the inevitable end of their lives and the failure to fulfill their youthful dreams. Though they hope for change, both the reader and audience know the reality of existence will make it impossible.

Concepts:

The repetition of concepts should also draw the literary detective's attention. The author is pointing again and again to something that the reader should not miss.

Through this kind of repetition, Ernest Hemingway indicates the motivation of a boxer who intentionally loses his final match in the short story ***Fifty-Grand.*** The protagonist, Jack Brennan, mentions his wife and/or family on almost every page. It is the financial security of his wife and family that motivates him. To secure a better

Chapter One	Chapter Seven
Daisy and Jordan lying on couches in white dresses	Daisy and Jordan lying on couches in white dresses
Tom on the phone with the Wilsons	Tom on the phone with the Wilsons
Daisy and Jordan's dresses are rippling and fluttering in a wind	Daisy and Jordan's dresses are moving in the breeze of a fan
Daisy's daughter is mentioned	Daisy's daughter is introduced
Gatsby is mentioned	Gatsby is present throughout

Table 1. In **The Great Gatsby**, readers who visited the Buchanan household in *Chapter One* return there in *Chapter Seven*

Chapter One	Chapter Seven
Animals huddle together to listen to Old Major's dream of Animal Farm	Animals huddle together at the knoll after the executions – Orwell tells the reader it reminds the animals of the way they huddled in Chapter One
Animals celebrate successful rebellion at the knoll	Animals lament failure of the dream of Animal Farm at the knoll
Animals sing "Beasts of England"	Animals sing "Beasts of England"
Hope and happiness throughout	Sadness and despair

Table 2. In *Animal Farm*, similarities between the two scenes serve to highlight the contrast

future for his family, he is willing to lose the match in order to win fifty thousand dollars. It is his family and not boxing that provides meaning to Jack Brennan's existence.

> *He didn't like being away from his wife and the kids, and he was sore and grouchy most of the time (394)....Jack was on the porch writing a letter to his wife (395)..."I'd a damn sight rather be in town with the wife" (396)..." I worry about the kids. I worry about the wife" (397).*

In her short story **Bliss**, Katherine Mansfield highlights (among other things) the societal restrictions inflicted on women by continuously pointing to *how idiotic civilization is*:

> *How idiotic civilization is! Why be given a body if you have to keep it shut up in a case like a rare, rare fiddle? ... [She]hung up the receiver, thinking how much more than idiotic civilization was.*

Arthur Miller's **Death of a Salesman** uses concept repetition to highlight Willy Loman's unrealistic expectations of being *well-liked*. The playwright also highlights the detrimental effect the teaching of this belief has on both of Willy Loman's sons.

> *...Charley is not – liked. He's liked, but he's not – well-liked ...Be liked and you will never want.*

Willy's son Happy learns this lesson well. He encourages his brother Biff in an unrealistic business venture based solely on the precept of being well-liked:

> *I bet he'd back you...You're well liked, Biff.*

Later in Act II, the character of Charley (Willy's only friend) comments upon the erroneous connection Willy makes with financial success and being well-liked:

*Why must everybody like you? Who liked J.P. Morgan?
Was he impressive? In a Turkish bath he'd look like a
butcher. But with his pockets on he was very well liked.*

Exercise at the Crime Scene

Words:

In the following section of T.S. Eliot's poem ***The Four Quartets,***
three key interconnected words should be immediately perceptible to
the good literary detective:

> *O dark dark dark. They all go into the dark/ The vacant
> interstellar spaces, the vacant into the vacant/ The captains,
> merchant bankers, eminent men of letters…all go into the
> dark…And we all go with them, into the silent funeral…*

1. What two words are noticeably repeated and how does the
   third principal word *funeral* suggest what the author is trying
   to highlight?

Scenes:

Compare the two scenes below, from John Steinbeck's novel ***Of
Mice and Men:***

Chapter One	Chapter Six
Idyllic descriptions of the Salinas River and Gabilan Mountains at the spot where George and Lennie are first introduced	Idyllic descriptions of the Salinas River and Gabilan Mountains at the spot where George and Lennie are first introduced
George and Lennie enter into the clearing, a heron flies away	Lennie, by himself, enters into the clearing, a heron kills and eats a snake
George and Lennie talk about their dreams for the future with a belief in its possibility	George and Lennie talk about their dreams for the future with George knowing it will never become a reality
George is looking out for Lennie	George is looking out for Lennie
A mouse has been killed	Lennie is killed by George to protect him from the cruel justice of vigilantes

A lot has happened in the lives of George and Lennie in the interval between Chapter One and Chapter Six. The contrasts and comparisons above illustrate that George and Lennie, two lifelong friends, will not be continuing their lives together (an important point for the two characters since the novel's beginning). Something horrible has happened: Lennie has accidentally killed a woman and is about to be caught and tortured to death by vigilantes. As a mercy killing, while helping Lennie to peacefully imagine their future together, George shoots Lennie in the back of the head.

1. Steinbeck has taken great pains to return the two main characters to the same spot where their adventure began. He then describes that same spot as unchanged. What might the author be suggesting about the great change that has occurred in the lives of these two men? When drawing your conclusion, don't forget to use the title of the novel as an additionally significant clue: *Of Mice and Men*.

Concepts:

Take a look at the following two scenes from John Steinbeck's novel *Of Mice and Men*. The first takes place in Chapter Three and involves a conversation between George and Slim:

> *"I ain't got no people," George said. "I seen the guys that go around on the ranches alone. That ain't no good. They don't have no fun. After a long time they get mean. They get wantin' to fight all the time."*
> *"Yeah, they get mean," Slim agreed. "They get so they don't want to talk to nobody."*

The second scene takes place in Chapter Four and involves an encounter between an African-American man named Crooks and Lennie, one of the novel's main characters:

> *"A guy needs somebody – to be near him." He [Crooks] whined, "A guy goes nuts if he ain't got nobody. Don't make no difference who the guy is, long's he's with you. I tell ya," he cried, "I tell ya a guy gets too lonely an' he gets sick."*

1. What is the concept that is being repeated? And what important lesson is the author trying to teach the reader?

Characterization

"I get a very vague idea of Mrs. Kingsley – that she is young, pretty, reckless, and wild. That she drinks and does dangerous things when she drinks. That she is a sucker for the men and might take up with a stranger who might turn out to be a crook."

Philip Marlowe**, *The Lady in the Lake***

Recreating the complexities of human beings in fictional characters is part of the important process of characterization. A detective will always increase an understanding of a case by gaining insight into the individuals involved in it. Through gaining an insight into the qualities and peculiarities of the people a story is about, the literary detective can also understand much about the actual story. Some of the focus areas of characterization are social status, beliefs, thoughts, experiences, occupation, dialect, age, gender, educational background, and cultural background.

In Mark Twain's short story ***A True Story, Repeated Word for Word as I Heard It***, the dialect or vernacular of a former slave named Aunt Rachel tells us something about her that the text does not.

> *Well, I thinks to myse'f, if my little Henry ever got a chance to run away, he'd make to de Norf, o' course. So one day I comes in dah whah de big officers was, in de parlor, an' I drops a kurtchy, so, an' I up an' tole 'em' bout my Henry.*

The vernacular of course derives from the deep south of the United States, but an expression like "I up an' tole 'em" suggests a lack of education. Recognizing the latter peculiarity in Aunt Rachel's dialect might lead to further historical research into the American pre-Civil War period. This research would verify that it was illegal to educate an African-American who was a slave.

As described by the author, the story's intent was to show readers the truth about slavery. This is accomplished through the story's vivid descriptions of such horrific events as the splitting up of a family during a slave auction. By understanding Aunt Rachel's lack of education, the literary detective gains an insight into yet another layer of the story's deeper meaning: African-Americans were also oppressed by being denied the right to an education.

The seditiousness of this law is highlighted in the reader's actual experience of reading the dialogue of an uneducated slave. Firstly, the difficulty in understanding the speech frustrates the reader and, in effect, recreates the frustration involved in communicating with such a person. Secondly, the speech of the uneducated slave serves to verify prejudicial pre-conceived notions of intelligence that existed in the 19th century. In the case of Mark Twain's runaway slave, Jim, in *The Adventures of Huckleberry Finn*, for example, readers may initially make the assumption that the character lacks intelligence because of the way he speaks. This attitude to Jim dissipates, of course, as (along with Huckleberry Finn) readers are forced to spend time with the runaway slave and witness, through many examples, the great intelligence that Jim does possess.

The characterization of the protagonist Harold Krebs in Ernest Hemingway's short story *Soldier's Home* provides a means for discovering the work's deeper meaning. Harold Krebs is a veteran of World War I who now refuses to pray and tells his Methodist Christian mother that he no longer lives in The Kingdom of God. The past experience of Harold, as a boy from a small Kansas town, who is a member of a practicing Christian family and used to be a pupil of a Methodist College, now stands in sharp contrast to the atheist he has become. His experiences as a soldier in five bloody battles, which are listed in the story, allow the literary detective to make the assumption that his war experience has changed him. As Krebs himself remarks, even though the town he returns to is the same, he has radically changed. This is emphasized in the story by Kreb's obvious depression, lethargy, and avoidance of everyone in the town.

Exercise at the Crime Scene

In James Joyce's short story *Eveline,* the protagonist of the same name is at a crossroads in her life. She is torn between staying in Dublin, Ireland to help look after her father and two young children, and going to Buenos Aires, Argentina with her lover. Near the end of the story, the narrator tells us: "...She prayed to God to direct her, to show her what was her duty..."

1. What does this one line reveal about Eveline's beliefs, thoughts, and cultural background?

That while Eveline may not have always followed God's word (based on the fact that she had a lover), she still believed in God and his influence on her life.

Setting

"On the east side of the hall a free stair case, tile-paved, rose to a gallery with a wrought-iron railing and another piece of stained-glass romance. Large hard chairs with rounded red plush seats were backed into the vacant spaces of the wall round about. They didn't look as if anybody had ever sat in them."

Philip Marlowe, ***The Big Sleep***

The scene or background of a work such as a play, movie, or narrative is important to the literary detective. Just as an actual detective will make certain observations of the place where a suspect lives or the locales in which the suspect likes to frequent, the literary detective will learn much about a work's theme through the places an author creates for a story.

In Emily Bronte's ***Wuthering Heights***, the author helps illustrate the conflict between Nature and Culture through the use of setting. *Wuthering Heights* is the name of the house that represents nature, as does Heathcliff, the man who lives there:

> *Wuthering Heights is the name of Mr. Heathcliff's dwelling. 'Wuthering' being a significant provincial adjective, descriptive of the atmospheric tumult to which its station is exposed in stormy weather. Pure, bracing ventilation they must have up there at all times, indeed: one may guess the power of the north wind, blowing over the edge, by the excessive slant of a few stunted firs at the end of the house; and by a range of gaunt thorns all stretching their limbs one way, as if craving alms of the sun.*

The mutilated trees and vegetation surrounding *Wuthering Heights* illustrate its contrast to *Thrushcross Grange,* the house that represents culture in the novel. Located in a soft valley below *Wuthering Heights, Thrushcross Grange* is protected from the winds of the high moorland. Life at the *Grange* is a life of soft luxury:

> *The light came from thence; they had not put up the shutters,*

and the curtains were only half closed...It was beautiful – a splendid place carpeted with crimson, and crimson-covered chairs and tables, and a pure white ceiling bordered by gold, a shower of glass-drops hanging in silver chains from the centre, and shimmering with little soft tapers.

In F. Scott Fitzgerald's **The Great Gatsby**, the waste produced by industrialization is reflected in the setting of what the novel calls "The Valley of Ashes." Located halfway between West Egg (a garishly wealthy part of Long Island) and New York, the Valley of Ashes is described as a *wasteland*:

...A fantastic farm where ashes grow like wheat into ridges and hills and grotesque gardens; where ashes take the forms of houses and chimneys and rising smoke and, finally, with a transcendent effort, of men who move dimly and already crumbling through the powdery air.

The lives of those who are forced by economics to live in the valley are wasted lives. They are victims of the wealth of America. George B. Wilson, who owns a gas station in the valley, is covered in the same white ashen dust that covers the entire area. When he walks away, the narrator tells us, he simply disappears and becomes just another part of the desolate surroundings.

Exercise at the Crime Scene

The setting for James Joyce's short story *Araby* is Dublin, Ireland in 1905. Historical research tells us that the region is politically charged with resentments arising from the English influence in Ireland. A young Irish boy has been looking forward to going to a bazaar called *Araby*. He expects to find a magical place that lives up to its name and all the romantic visions that the Middle East held for Europeans at the time. His reason for going there is to buy an exotic gift for a girl, he believes, he loves. However, after passing through a *ruinous* part of town, he finds a warehouse that is veiled in darkness and disturbingly silent. Instead of having exotic wares from the Middle East for sale, the actual bazaar is run by rude English stall owners who are selling English tea sets and porcelain vases. He will not be able to buy the exotic gift for his friend's older sister, which he has convinced himself will be the beginning of their romantic relationship.

1. How does the setting that James Joyce creates help illustrate the story's deeper theme of dream versus reality?

Staples of Interpretation

"Intuition is like reading a word without having to spell it out. A child can't do that, because it has had so little experience. But a grown-up person knows the word because he's seen it often before."
Miss Jane Marple, **Murder at the Vicarage**

Much like words you instantly recognize because of frequent exposure to them, the following *Staples of Interpretation* are techniques that many diverse writers have used in similar ways.

Epigraphs:

Along with the title, the quotation with which the author chooses to open his or her work is one of the most direct means of informing the reader of hidden meaning.

In Ernest Hemingway's *For Whom the Bell Tolls*, the author encourages the world to get actively involved in the war against Fascism by supporting the Republicans in Spain. Viewing the Spanish Civil War as a precursor to World War II, the novel presents the Spanish fight as the world's fight. In this way, the American Robert Jordan sacrifices his life because he shares in the Spanish sacrifice to destroy Fascism. The novel's title is quoted from a poem by John Donne, which emphasizes that one man's death is every man's experience and, therefore, not isolated:

> *No man is an Iland, intire of it selfe; every man is a peece of the Continent, a part of the maine; if a Clod bee washed away by the Sea, Europe is the lesse, as well as if a Promontorie were, as well as if a Mannor of thy friends or of thine owne were; any mans death diminishes me, because I am involved in Mankinde; And therefore never send to know for whom the bell tolls; It tolls for thee.*

As mentioned in the section *Tools of the Trade*, research on the author is also useful when studying works – especially when arguing that Hemingway's novel had a political agenda. Ernest Hemingway participated actively in the Spanish civil war as both a reporter and advocate for the Loyalist cause. He narrated as well as wrote the commentary for *The Spanish Earth*, a documentary film designed to increase public support for the Loyalists in Spain.

The epigraph for ***The Great Gatsby*** also provides a clue to one of the novel's themes –living too long with a single dream:

> *Then wear the gold hat, if that will move her; If you can*
> *bounce high, bounce for her too, Till she cry "Lover,*
> *gold-hatted, high-bouncing lover, I must have you!"*

Never giving up on a dream that is unrealistic and will ultimately destroy you is the tragic theme behind the protagonist Jay Gatsby. As a man of great potential, Gatsby in his tragedy is also suggestive of the larger national tragedy: the great and idealized potential of the United States has also been destroyed by the pursuit of money and material acquisitions. The novel's epigraph was so important to F. Scott Fitzgerald that he wrote it himself and then disguised it by accrediting it to a pseudonym, *Thomas Parke D'Invilliers*.

The Sun Also Rises, Ernest Hemingway's quintessential novel of the lost generation (the generation of men and women who came of age during the First World War, 1914-18), reveals its subject in an epigraph attributed to Gertrude Stein:

> *You are all a lost generation.*

Seasons:

Many works will signal events to come by indicating a particular season. This serves to evoke the imagery that each represents.

- *Spring*: the season of hope and optimism
- *Summer*: the season of bounty
- *Fall*: the slow decline or demise of living things
- *Winter*: the season of stagnation and death

In ***The Great Gatsby***, the narrator (Nick Carraway) arrives in the East during spring. Nick's youthful expectations of professional success perfectly match the season of hope and optimism. In summer, the season of bounty, the relationships that make up the novel develop. In the autumn, Jay Gatsby dies and Nick ends his love affair with Jordan Baker and returns to the West.

T.S. Eliot's poem *The Waste Land* uses knowledge of the seasons to show not only the tragic nature of existence, but also life itself as a wasted hope. In this case, the season of hope becomes the cruellest month. This is because all hope is doomed in a life that is, ultimately, born to end in death.

> *April is the cruelest month, breeding*
> *Lilacs out of the dead land, mixing*
> *Memory and desire, stirring*
> *Dull roots with spring rain (1-5).*

The Age of Thirty:

It is an accepted sociological theory that the early thirties are a time when individuals will re-evaluate their life situation. The purpose of this re-evaluation is to determine whether the dreams of youth are still realistically achievable or not. If not, the individual must change goals now before it is too late. The age of thirty, then, is also symbolic of a transition into adulthood. This transition is marked by self-awareness and the acceptance of responsibility for one's actions.

In *The Great Gatsby*, Nick does what all the other more immature characters fail to do: he becomes self-aware. The transition takes place after Nick's thirtieth birthday:

> *I was thirty. Before me stretched the portentous, menacing*
> *road of a new decade…Thirty – the promise of a decade of*
> *loneliness, a thinning list of single men to know, a thinning*
> *brief-case of enthusiasm, thinning hair.*

When Nick is accused of misleading his ex-lover, he accepts the responsibility for his actions:

"I'm thirty," I said. "I'm five years too old to lie to myself and call it honor…She didn't answer. Angry, and half in love with her, and tremendously sorry, I turned away.

With the character of Biff in **Death of a Salesman,** self-awareness is also connected to the early thirties:

I'm thirty-four years old, I oughta be makin' my future…I'm like a boy. I'm not married, I'm not in business, I just – I'm like a boy.

Later in Act II, Biff will take responsibility for his mistakes and insist on dealing with the facts of not only his own life, but also the lives of his family members:

…I realized what a ridiculous lie my whole life has been! We've been talking in a dream for fifteen years.

The Significance of Mirrors:

A mirror is often used to subtly describe the physical traits of a character to a reader. Yet, it also provides the author with a way to explore self-awareness. Though we take it for granted (especially in modern times with the advent of photography and video recorders), the mirror was once the only accessible means – and remains, to this day, the most accessible means – through which we can view ourselves as others see us. Often, our desire to escape complete self-awareness forces us to manipulate the image in order to create the most positive impression. Whether it is through the use of pink mirrors or simply by posing in just the right way, it is the image we wish to project that we desire to see in the mirror. At any rate, when a character looks in a mirror it is often a motif for self-awareness. This is especially true if the act is not immediately followed by a physical description or if the reader is already aware of the individual's physical characteristics.

When the protagonist in Virginia Woolf's **Mrs. Dalloway** looks in the mirror, she reveals an awareness of the many roles she has and will play in her lifetime. All these roles, she tells us, make up the composite parts of her self.

> *She had just broken into her fifty-second year…How*
> *many million times she had seen her face, and always with*
> *the same imperceptible contraction! She pursed her lips*
> *when she looked in the glass. It was to give her face point…*
> *That was her self when some effort, some call on her to be*
> *her self, drew the parts together, she alone knew how different,*
> *how incompatible and composed so for the world only into one*
> *centre, one diamond, one woman who sat in her drawing-room*
> *and made a meeting-point…*

In Katherine Mansfield's ***Bliss,*** an oppressed woman is frightened of the emotional consequences that awareness of her situation might cause. As the title suggests, *ignorance is bliss*:

> *She hardly dared to look into the cold mirror – but she did*
> *look, and it gave her back a woman, radiant, with smiling,*
> *trembling lips, with big, dark eyes and an air of listening,*
> *waiting for something…divine to happen…that she knew*
> *must happen…infallibly.*

The above passage describes some of the woman's physical characteristics. Yet, with all its implications, it also provides an insight into an individual who hesitates to view herself in a mirror.

Names:

The name an author gives to a character is also an access point into meaning. Caricatures meant to represent types are often given satirical names. This indicates the author's attitude toward a recognized group of people.

The famous heroine of William Thackeray's ***Vanity Fair*** is called Becky Sharp. Known for her ability to manipulate others, Becky Sharp is highly intelligent and cunning. In a word, she is *sharp*.

In ***The Great Gatsby,*** F. Scott Fitzgerald uses the crude and ugly sounding names of Gatsby's guests to allude to the unsavoury nature of the people who frequent his parties. As caricatures, they too are meant to suggest types rather than actual individuals. Along with being crude, many of the names evoke racist or sexually explicit slang words.

> ...Hornbeams...Willie Voltaires, and a whole clan named Blackbuck...and Edgar Beaver...and the Ripley Snells...

Arthur Miller's **Death of a Salesman** uses the name of the playwright's main character (Willy Loman, or "Low man") to suggest his low social status as well as his low self-worth. As Biff Loman later states, the Lomans are examples of the average American – they are *a dime a dozen*. The play's social statement is clear: the average American is viewed and treated in a low, demeaning way. This fact is made more tragic by the realization that average Americans also share this demeaning view of their own social class.

Much like the main character in Katherine Mansfield's short story **Bliss**, Happy Loman's happiness in **Death of a Salesman** is attributed to his unawareness:

> He, like his brother [Biff], is lost, but in a different way, for he has never allowed himself to turn his face toward defeat and is thus more confused and hard-skinned, although seemingly more content.

The name *Happy*, then, is an ironic one. The author means to show that happiness based on lies is a false happiness. Since he has purposely remained unaware of his failures and shortcomings, he does not have to deal with the negative feelings attached to them. As a consequence, Happy Loman will never make an attempt to improve his life situation.

Another character whose name is significant in Miller's play is Dave Singleman. Dave Singleman, unlike Willy Loman, is a successful salesman. Willy Loman longs to "be remembered and loved and helped" the way Dave Singleman is by his clientele. However, as Singleman's name suggests, Willy is remembered, loved, and helped in a way that Dave Singleman is not: by both a wife and family. The argument of Dave Singleman's marital status is made solely on the character's last name.

It takes time and hard work to become a successful salesman, time away from family and friends. Arthur Miller illustrates that Willy Loman is a success where Dave Singleman is not – in his personal life. It is for the reader to decide which kind of success is better: professional or personal.

Exercise at the Crime Scene

Epigraphs:

1. Match the numbered epigraphs with the corresponding letter of the correct summary:

   i. _____ "Did I request thee, Maker, from my clay / To mould me man? Did I solicit thee / From darkness to promote me?"

   Paradise Lost

   ii. _____ "It is certain my Conviction gains infinitely, the moment another soul will believe in it."

   Novalis

   iii. _____ "Verily, verily, I say unto you, except a corn of wheat fall into the ground and die, it abideth alone: but if it die, it bringeth forth much fruit."

   St. John XII.24

Summary:

A. ***The Brothers Karamazov,*** by Fyodor Dostoevsky, is a portrait of Russian society in the 1870s. Following the Karamazov family, the main underlying theme of the novel is redemption through suffering.

B. *Lord Jim,* by Joseph Conrad, tells the story of a young man who, after an isolated act of cowardice, loses all faith in himself until a group of island natives has faith in him. One of the underlying themes is the potential lives each of us possess, yet, never realize.

C. *Frankenstein,* by Mary Shelley, is the story of a scientist who creates a monster in an experiment. He later rejects the monster he created. One of the underlying themes is the societal dangers of playing God with technology.

Names:

1. Match each lettered descriptive sentence with its corresponding name below:

_____ Jake Barnes
_____ Mr. Gradgrind
_____ Jack Thriftless
_____ Cheeryble Brothers
_____ Mrs. Mantrap

A. a woman who ensnares men like prey
B. a man who owes *money in every capital in Europe.*
C. a cruel schoolmaster
D. always looking on the good side of things

2. Which of the above names did you not select? Why?

Associative Pairing

"...We must take notice of Peculiar Things...It reminds me of the time the man went round pretending to be the gas inspector...Quite a little haul he got...It is a Peculiar Thing."
                    Miss Jane Marple, **Murder at the Vicarage**

The human mind automatically pairs and associates. In psychology, the phenomenon known as classical conditioning (pairing stimuli such as food with a reinforcer such as money) results from this natural tendency. In order to cope with myriad stimuli, the brain also stores relevant information in categories that utilize associations. Miss Jane Marple was famous for her use of associations in solving crimes. The writer will use this natural tendency to advantage by continually using *associative pairings*.

In **The Great Gatsby** there are a number of these kinds of pairings. One of the most important, however, is the way in which the narrator is always mentioning the sound of Daisy's voice whenever she speaks.

> *...There was an excitement in her voice that men who had cared for her found difficult to forget: a singing compulsion, a whispered "Listen," a promise that she had done gay, exciting things just a while since and that there were gay, exciting things hovering in the next hour...I think that voice (Daisy's) held him most, with its fluctuating, feverish warmth, because it couldn't be over-dreamed – that voice was a deathless song.*

Later in the novel, Jay Gatsby will reveal to the reader that the fascination with Daisy's voice is related to the theme of the novel – the power of money.

> *"Her voice is full of money," he [Gatsby] said suddenly. That was it. I'd never understood it before. It was full of money – that was the inexhaustible charm that rose and fell in it, the*

jingle of it, the cymbals' song of it...High in a white palace the
king's daughter, the golden girl...

Another subtler associative pairing in the novel involves the
automobile. An American symbol of wealth and stature, the car also
becomes a symbol of destruction in the novel through associative
pairing.

In the ditch beside the road, right side up, but violently shorn
of one wheel, rested a new coupe which had left Gatsby's
drive not two minutes before.

Later in the novel, Nick highlights the important connection between
careless driving and careless people:

It was on that same house-party that we had a curious
conversation about driving a car. It started because she
passed so close to some workman that our fender flicked a
button on one man's coat. "You're a rotten driver," I [Nick]
protested. "Either you ought to be more careful, or you
oughtn't to drive at all...Suppose you met somebody just
as careless as yourself."

Finally, at the novel's end, the automobile is connected to the tragic
deaths of three people – including the protagonist, Jay Gatsby.

In Katherine Mansfield's short story **Bliss,** a suspicion that the
protagonist's husband is having an affair with her friend, Pearl
Fulton, is acquired through associative pairing. Every time the
protagonist mentions her husband, Pearl Fulton is also mentioned.
This, coupled with her husband's obviously feigned and negative
attitude toward Pearl Fulton, helps the literary detective suspect the
affair before it is revealed:

[Harry] voted her dullish, and "cold like all blonde women,
with a touch, perhaps, of anaemia of the brain"...He made
a point of catching Bertha's heels with replies of that kind.

Both her husband and Pearl Fulton are conspicuously late for the party Bertha is giving. When her husband finally arrives, Bertha is suddenly reminded of Pearl Fulton's absence.

> *She talked and laughed and positively forgot until he had come in (just as she had imagined) that Pearl Fulton had not turned up.*

Through the use of associative pairings, the same unconfirmed suspicions that the story's heroine (Bertha) experiences are reproduced in the reader – the story's heroine suspects, but without real proof tries to ignore it. The reader also suspects, but cannot be certain of the fact until Bertha is made certain of it at the story's end. Once again, the author highlights what her title suggests – *ignorance is bliss.*

Exercise at the Crime Scene

Associative Pairing:

In the following excerpts from Tennessee William's play *A Streetcar Named Desire*, Blanche Dubois's memories of the past are consistently paired with *Varsouviana* polka music.

> *STANLEY: You were married once, weren't you? [The music of the polka rises up, faint in the distance].*
>
> *BLANCHE: Yes. When I was quite young.*
>
> *STANLEY: What happened?*
>
> *BLANCHE: The boy – the boy died. [She sinks back down] I'm afraid I'm – going to be sick! [Her head falls on her arms].*
> *(Sc. 1.)*

Later in Scene vi, as the polka once again plays in the background, Blanche reveals that the *Varsouviana* music is connected to the suicide of her young husband:

> BLANCHE: *We danced the Varsouviana! Suddenly in the middle of the dance the boy I had married broke away from me and ran out of the casino. A few moments later – a shot!*

> *[The polka stops abruptly. Blanche rises stiffly. Then, the polka resumes in a major key.]*

> BLANCHE: *...It was because – on the dance-floor – unable to stop myself – I'd suddenly said – "I saw! I know! You disgust me..."*

The playwright then sets up the beginning of Scene ix in the following way:

> *...On the table beside the chair is a bottle of liquor and a glass. The rapid, feverish polka tune, the "Varsouviana," is heard. The music is in her mind; she is drinking to escape it and the sense of disaster closing in on her, and she seems to whisper the words of the song.*

Later in the same scene, when she realizes her past indiscretions have destroyed the possibilities of a future with a suitor, she tells him:

> BLANCHE: *I'll just – [She touches her forehead vaguely. The polka tune starts up again.] – pretend I don't notice anything different about you! That – music again...*

And near the end of Scene ix:

> *[The polka tune fades in.]*
> BLANCHE *[as if to herself]: Crumble and fade and – regrets –recriminations... "If you'd done this, it wouldn't've cost me that!"*

Finally, at the play's end while Blanche Dubois is being taken against her will to an insane asylum, the playwright's notes tell us that the *Varsouviana* is played in the background through a "weird distortion."

1. What possible deductions can you make about the pairing of the polka with the character of Blanche Dubois?

2. If one would assert that guilt and self-hate create a negative force in Blanche Dubois's life, how could you use the *Varsouviana* polka as evidence?

Page Space

"He was a big man but not more than six feet five inches tall and not wider than a beer truck...If he had been a smaller man and more quietly dressed, I might have thought he was going to pull a stick-up."

Philip Marlowe, ***Farewell My Lovely***

Sometimes, size does matter! Since space is limited, especially in modern literature, writers must use it wisely. The actual physical space that a writer gives to a certain idea is often an indication of importance. The reader should look closely at any paragraph that takes up more space than usual.

In ***Death of a Salesman***, Arthur Miller takes up an entire page to give the reader some insight into why it is so important for Willy Loman to be a salesman. It is the longest speech in the play and just by looking at it the literary detective knows that if Miller is willing to give the speech that much space it must be important. It is in this speech that the reader learns Willy Loman is a man who yearns to be *remembered, loved and helped.*

When F. Scott Fitzgerald introduces *The Valley of Ashes* in ***The Great Gatsby***, the reader can anticipate future symbolic importance by the amount of space used on the physical page. A full page is given over to its description and location, and to a billboard (prominently situated in the valley) that shows the eyes of Doctor T.J. Eckleburg. By the novel's end, all of these things are revealed as major symbols.

Exercise at the Crime Scene

Look at the following dialogue from Arthur Miller's play ***Death of a Salesman.*** The literary detective would immediately perceive one part of the dialogue scene as potentially important evidence.

HAPPY: What do you mean?

BIFF: Never mind. Just don't lay it all to me.

HAPPY: But I think if you just got started – I mean – is there any future for you out there?

BIFF: I tell ya, Hap, I don't know what the future is. I don't know – what I'm supposed to want.

HAPPY: What do you mean?

BIFF: Well, I spent six or seven years after high school trying to work myself up. Shipping clerk, salesman, business of one kind or another. And it's a measly manner of existence. To get on that subway on the hot mornings in summer. To devote your whole life to keeping stock, or making phone calls, or selling or buying. To suffer fifty weeks of the year for the sake of a two-week vacation, when all you really desire is to be outdoors, with your shirt off. And always to have to get ahead of the next fella. And still – that's how you build a future.

1. By observing the use of page space alone, which part of the dialogue do you think is the most important?

2. Why might this passage be important to the understanding of Biff's character?

Biographical Research

"...I'm a licensed private investigator and have been for quite a while. I'm a lone wolf, unmarried, getting middle-aged, and not rich. I've been in jail more than once and I don't do divorce business. I like liquor and women and chess and a few other things...I'm a native son, born in Santa Rosa, both parents dead, no brothers or sisters, and when I get knocked off in a dark alley sometime, if it happens, as it could to anyone in my business, and to plenty of people in any business or no business at all these days, nobody will feel that the bottom has dropped out of his or her life."

Philip Marlow, The Long Goodbye

As alluded to in *Tools of the Trade,* an investigation into the author's life and experience is an essential part of a literary detective's preliminary examination of a text. In all cases, biographical research is an important component in unpacking the deepest layers of a literary work; in some cases, it is an absolute necessity.

An excellent example of this is the author Ernest Hemingway, who believed that literature was rooted in a writer's own personal experience. While acknowledging that fictional aspects are put into a work by the writer in order to round the story out and give it life, the great American author stated that the core of each work is made up out of what the author knows. He told his editor Maxwell Perkins that "whatever success I have had has been through writing what I know about" (*Selected Letters*).

However, the essential aspect of biographical research for Hemingway and many other writers is not only based in knowledge of the writer's personal experiences, but also, and many times more importantly, in the world view or personal philosophy that those experiences created.

In the case of Ernest Hemingway, without understanding his personal philosophy for life, the reader cannot hope to gain a full and complete understanding of his work. The famous Hemingway Hero is rooted in this philosophy, as is the even more well known characteristic behind the author's concept of courage, which he called *grace under pressure*.

The short story **Indian Camp**, published by the author in his first short story collection, **In Our Time**, contains a passage that demands understanding if the deepest layer of the story is to be uncovered. As the story is multi-layered, a reader can still, without biographical research, access much of the more obvious meaning embedded in the text: a young boy is beginning his journey to adulthood through a series of initiations, which in this case is precipitated by his physician father, who takes his son to observe the delivery of a child. One obvious feature of the story that illustrates the theme is that the boy enters the story in his father's arms and proceeds to ask childish questions to his father as he prepares to deliver the baby. At the end of the story, the boy no longer sits in his father's arms and his questions have matured into existential inquiries.

While the above provides for a rich discussion of the text, one important scene remains enigmatic without an understanding of the author's philosophy on manhood and courage. The doctor soon discovers that the child is dangerously in a breech presentation and, even though the doctor is without the necessary tools or anaesthetic in the remote environment of an Indian reserve, he must perform an emergency Caesarian section. As his own terrified child watches and begs his father to give the struggling woman *something to make her stop screaming*, the father tells his son, "No. I haven't any anaesthetic…But her screams are not important. I don't hear them because they are not important."

The response of the father, to the chaotic situation he finds himself in, demonstrates the courage that Hemingway believed individuals needed to impose upon a world that operates at random, a world where individuals are often victims to the vicissitudes of life. By using his skill as a doctor to provide form to chaos and by having the courage to transcend his fear of the event and apply that knowledge, the doctor demonstrates the necessary qualities of manhood to his son, which is *grace under pressure*. Contrarily, the woman's husband, who is also present at the same moment, is unable to confront the situation with courage and instead finds refuge in escape by suicide.

While a theme of the collection and the story itself, involves the transition from childhood to adulthood, the story operates at a much deeper level when the implications of the above scene are recognized and understood: The transition from childhood to adulthood is only one part of an individual's maturation process; while this will involve complex life experiences, it can also involve such mundane occurrences as the many physical changes individuals will go through, which are both natural and inevitable. The more important matter then is not an inquiry into how a child becomes an adult, but rather the complexities involved in what kind of adult a child will become.

In the case of ***Indian Camp***, the reader is faced with two options as personified by both the woman's husband and the doctor: one handles the challenges of life through avoidance and escape, while the other confronts these same challenges and, in so doing, transcends them. A study of Hemingway's works will reveal to the reader the many characteristics inherent in both kinds of individuals; in the process, the author gives the reader the essential ingredients to become what is now known as *The Hemingway Hero*.

Without an understanding of Hemingway's personal philosophy as an introduction to the text, the above would remain largely inaccessible to the reader; furthermore, an understanding of the writer's own struggles with depression and suicide will also serve to enrich a reader's sensitivity to the many layers of meaning presented in his work.

Simple Detective Work

"They say that genius is an infinite capacity for taking pains," he remarked with a smile. "It's a very bad definition, but it does apply to detective work."

Sherlock Holmes, ***A Study In Scarlet***

Good detective work demands awareness and attention to detail. The good detective sees clues where others do not. Presented in its current format, it is easy to identify the importance of all of the above. Presented in its proper context, however, the clues do not appear so conspicuously. In order to maximize impact, the writer must deliver the work's message with subtlety. A keen eye, the patience to reread and mark possible clues for later comparison is, often, the difference between a good reader and a bad reader. Just like the detective, the reader must be on the lookout for clues or he or she will miss them.

In the following paragraph from ***Animal Farm,*** George Orwell inserts a word that should give the literary detective a clue to the potential importance of the event:

> *Napoleon took no interest in Snowball's committees. He said that the education of the young was more important than anything that could be done for those who were already grown up. It happened that Jessie and Bluebell had both whelped soon after the hay harvest, giving birth between them to nine sturdy puppies. As soon as they were weaned Napoleon took them away from their mothers, saying that he would make himself responsible for their education. He took them up into a loft which could only be reached by a ladder from the harness-room, and there kept them in such seclusion that the rest of the farm soon forgot their existence.*

Did you identify the key word? Changing that one key word in the paragraph greatly impacts the future implications of the scene:

Napoleon took no interest in Snowball's committees. He said that the education of the young was more important than anything that could be done for those who were already grown up. It happened that Jessie and Bluebell had both whelped soon after the hay harvest, giving birth between them to nine sickly puppies. As soon as they were weaned Napoleon took them away from their mothers, saying that he would make himself responsible for their education. He took them up into a loft which could only be reached by a ladder from the harness-room, and there kept them in such seclusion that the rest of the farm soon forgot their existence.

Even though you may not have been acutely aware of the location of the key word (as intended by the author) it had its desired effect. The uneasy sense of urgency in Napoleon taking the puppies is the result of the reader either consciously or unconsciously noticing the fact that they were *sturdy*. The reader at some level understands that nine sturdy puppies will grow up to be nine very strong dogs.

*Napoleon took no interest in Snowball's committees. He said that the education of the young was more important than anything that could be done for those who were already grown up. It happened that Jessie and Bluebell had both whelped soon after the hay harvest, giving birth between them to nine **sturdy** puppies. As soon as they were weaned Napoleon took them away from their mothers, saying that he would make himself responsible for their education. He took them up into a loft which could only be reached by a ladder from the harness-room, and there kept them in such seclusion that the rest of the farm soon forgot their existence.*

Exercise at the Crime Scene

Read the following excerpt from F. Scott Fitzgerald's novel *The Great Gatsby*. The narrator, Nick Carroway, is describing, at the novel's end, his memory of West Egg, New York:

I see it as a night scene by El Greco: a hundred houses, at once conventional and grotesque, crouching under a sullen, overhanging sky and a lustreless moon. In the foreground four solemn men in dress suits are walking along the sidewalk with a stretcher on which lies a drunken woman in a white evening dress. Her hand, which dangles over the side, sparkles cold with jewels. Gravely the men turn in at a house – the wrong house. But no one knows the woman's name, and no one cares.

1. What is your reaction to the above excerpt?

2. The description above, in one way, seems very glamorous – a young woman in white evening dress is being carried by four well-dressed men. Yet, is there anything about the event that creates concern? If so, what?

3. What words or key information in the above description allude to the potential seriousness of the event? Why?

Case Closed

"As the strong man exults in his physical ability, delighting in such exercises as call his muscles into action, so glories the analyst in that moral activity which disentangles. He derives pleasure from even the most trivial occupations bringing his talents into play. He is fond of enigmas, of conundrums, of hieroglyphics; exhibiting in his solutions of each a degree of acumen which appears to the ordinary apprehension preternatural. His results, brought about by the very soul and essence of method, have, in truth, the whole air of intuition."

C. Auguste Dupin, The Purloined Letter

The wonder of great literature is that *no two people read the same work*. As explained in the section on Associative Pairing, individuals perceive the world through individual templates. These templates work upon the external stimuli that inundate an individual and filter out innumerable sources of relatively unimportant information. It is, however, the information that each individual is conditioned to select that affects the individual's interpretation. A humanist will most likely make a humanist interpretation of a John Donne poem that a feminist would view as feminist. Understanding the psychology behind human experience, good writers will allow individuals space for their own perceptual templates. This also explains why you can read works like these again and again and find something new each time. The work always has relevance to the reader, because it is constructed to be able to enter the reader's life experience at any given time. The writer always has access to the reader's psyche. The realist is able to view Jay Gatsby as a fool for sacrificing his life to an untrue woman at the same time that the romantic is able to applaud it as proof of man's capacity to dream. The individual who was a romantic as a teenager discovers something new when he or she later reads the novel as an adult who has become a realist. F. Scott Fitzgerald is able to produce a common understanding by tying this space together with the novel's main theme, which is unmistakable: obsession with money and material acquisitions has turned the American Dream into a nightmare.

The largest part of the study of English Literature is this space which allows for interpretation and all its creative possibilities. It is this space that allows for the reinvention and reinterpretation of a work's unmistakable themes. To effectively understand these works and have them provide meaning, the reader must be able to utilize the work's details in order to creatively interpret the information. It is this process that generates meaning and it is in this way that the study of great literary works becomes an art form. That is the method involved in good literary detection.

Answers To The Exercises

Page 23
The Title (Possible Deductions)

1.
- The word *Courage* in **The Red Badge of *Courage***: The attraction of war for many young men is having a theatre in which they can display their *courage*. This is true in the case of the novel's protagonist, Henry Fleming.

- The word *Red* in **The *Red* Badge of Courage**: The colour of blood is red, associated with wounds of warfare and death.

- The word *Badge* in **The Red *Badge* of Courage**: The symbol of bravery in actual warfare is not the tin decorations given out by a soldier's superiors. The symbol of bravery is, in actuality, the wounds, sometimes mortal, that one inflicts and incurs. In the case of Henry Fleming, his *red badge* of *courage* is a head injury.

Notice that the literary detective focuses on the three principal words in the title: *Red, Badge,* and *Courage*. The literary detective then tries to come up with a theory to explain their significance. Once the book has been read, further collected evidence will either support or refute the original theory regarding the title.

2. As stated above, the word *Red* in **The *Red* Badge of Courage** represents the red colour of blood.

Pages 28-29
Introduction of Characters

Essential Characteristics: (Possible Deduction)

1. At the very least there seems to be a certain amount of stress and depression in the individual. By novel's end this initial deduction will prove correct, as the character will end his life by suicide.

2.

> "If personality is an unbroken series of successful gestures, then there was something **ugly** about him, some heightened **insensitivity** to the promises of life, as if he were related to one of those intricate machines that register earthquakes ten thousand miles away. This responsiveness…was an extraordinary gift for **despair**, a(n) **unromantic** readiness such as I have never found in any other person and which it is not likely I shall ever find again."

Device: (Possible Deduction)

1. Steinbeck points out that, even in an open space, where it is not necessary, one of the individuals follows the other. This suggests that, in terms of their relationship, the man in front is the leader and the man in back is the follower. Just in that one sentence, an important dynamic in this relationship is revealed. One is dominant over the other: one is the leader and the other the follower. The rest of the chapter will establish this characteristic of their relationship, with all its nuances, even more.

Page 31
Establishing Genre

1. Some of the most popular forms are: *poetry, drama (plays), short*

stories, novellas, one-act plays, and *novels.*

Pages 38-40
<u>Repetition</u>

Words:

1. The word *dark* is repeated five times in the section and four times in the first sentence. The word *vacant* is repeated three times in the second sentence. When the literary detective connects these repeated words to the use of the word *funeral* (*dark, vacant, funeral*), he or she can instantly understand what the passage clearly states: We all die, and death is a vast or vacant nothingness.

Scenes: (Possible Deduction)

1. The world is ultimately indifferent to the lives and desires of individual human beings. Our problems, our dreams, our life, our death, are as significant to the workings of the natural world as the death of a single mouse is in the lives of men. As further illustrated in the Robert Burns poem from which John Steinbeck culled his title, "the best laid schemes of mice and men" are equally unimportant.

Concepts: (Possible Deduction)

1. The concept being repeated is loneliness. The author is trying to show the reader the negative consequences of being alone, without friends or family. One of the most important life lessons given in the entire book is the importance of friendship. In the above scenes, the author highlights this importance by telling readers what happens to individuals who are friendless.

Page 43
Characterization (Possible Deduction)

1. Since she prays, she must be a religious person or, at the very least, part of a religious culture. The setting of the story is Dublin, and the house she lives in has a "coloured print of the promises made to Blessed Margaret Mary Alacoque." This suggests she is from a Catholic background. Her use of the word *duty* also suggests that a sense of or adherence to duty is an important part of her self-image. At the story's end, Eveline stays in Dublin – one of the reasons being a promise she had made in the past to her dying mother. Eveline is trapped by her sense of duty.

Pages 45-46
Setting (Possible Deduction)

1. What the boy desires, expects, and dreams of concerning the bazaar is obliterated by the reality of the place. It is not the exotic event or locale he had expected. The setting Joyce creates reveals to both the reader and the boy one of adulthood's great lessons: There is usually a difference between dream and reality, between what you expect to accomplish and what you will actually accomplish.

Pages 53-54
Staples of Interpretation

Epigraphs:

1.

i.   __C__ "Did I request thee, Maker, from my clay / To
             mould me man? Did I solicit thee / From darkness to
             promote me?"

                                              Paradise Lost

ii.   __B__ "It is certain my Conviction gains infinitely, the
             moment another soul will believe in it."

                                                    Novalis

iii.   __A__ "Verily, verily, I say unto you, except a corn of
             wheat fall into the ground and die, it abideth alone:
             but if it die, it bringeth forth much fruit."

                                              St. John XII.24

Names:

1.

        _____   Jake Barnes
        __C__   Mr. Gradgrind
        __B__   Jack Thriftless
        __D__   Cheeryble Brothers
        __A__   Mrs. Mantrap

2. Jake Barnes possesses the qualities of an average name and,
    therefore, is meant to reflect a real individual with all the
    complexities of a real individual.

Pages 57-59
Associative Pairing

1. From the first pairing, which immediately follows a question
    about her dead husband, we can deduce that the polka has some
    significance to her tragic first marriage. This is later confirmed in
    Scene vi, when Blanche reveals that on the night of the suicide
    they were dancing to a *Varsouviana* polka. Yet, because it is

consistently paired with Blanche's emotional problems in the present, neither the music nor the suicidal incident it is paired with has been left entirely in Blanche's past. This tragic incident continues to be relevant in the present and, therefore, the future of Blanche Dubois.

2. Guilt from the past affects her present day-to-day life and is the catalyst for her many destructive life choices and self-loathing. At the moments in the play when this is made most clear, the *Varsouviana* is consistently heard. It is something she wishes to escape. Yet, due to her actions, it is something that imprisons her. In times of emotional turmoil, the music and its attached memory drive Blanche deeper into depression as well as emotional instability.

Pages 60-61
Page Space

1. According to the use of page space, the eye is immediately attracted to the largest paragraph where Biff describes his dissatisfaction with past jobs and how it confuses his goals for the future.

2. Biff's speech tells the audience what his problem is and why he has been unable to do anything productive in his life. The character is trying to define success. If success is money, then he should work at a job he does not like to achieve it. In this way, exchanging fifty weeks of the year for money is a good investment. However, if success is actually happiness, then he would be a failure to work at something that makes him miserable. Until he can satisfactorily find an answer to this question, Biff's character will remain stagnant as he will be unable to make a productive life decision.

Pages 67-68
<u>Simple Detective Work</u>

2. Yes, four men are carrying an incapacitated woman into a house that is not her own, without witnesses and with no one to be concerned about her whereabouts.

3.

    i.   *Drunken woman:* Since the woman is drunk, she is unable to protect herself or understand what is happening to her.

    ii.   *Wrong house*: The house she is being taken to is not her house.

    iii.   *No one knows the woman's name*: Either none of the men carrying her know who she is, or anyone that might be witnessing the incident is ignorant of her identity.

    iv.   *No one cares*: Since no one cares, anything can happen.

    v.   Observation of the key words used at the beginning of the excerpt also suggest something of an unsettling or dark nature: *grotesque, sullen, crouching, lustreless, solemn.*

It is unclear just what the author is suggesting about the woman's predicament. Yet, for the reasons described above, any reader would be uncomfortable with the situation if someone they loved were in the drunken woman's position.

Works Cited

Bronte, Emily. <u>Wuthering Heights.</u> New York: Random House, 1945.

Chandler, Raymond. <u>Farewell My Lovely</u>. New York: Alfred A. Knopf, 1940.

Chandler, Raymond. <u>The Long Goodbye</u>. Hamish Hamilton, 1953.

Christie, Agatha. <u>The Mysterious Affair at Styles</u>. New York: John Lane Co., 1920.

Christie, Agatha. <u>Murder at the Vicarage</u>. New York: Dodd, Mead & Co. 1930.

Eliot, T. S. <u>The Waste Land</u>. New York: Boni & Liveright, 1922.

Fitzgerald, F. Scott. <u>The Great Gatsby</u>. New York: Charles Scribner's Sons, 1925.

Hemingway, Ernest. "Indian Camp" from <u>In Our Time</u>. New York: Charles Scribner's Sons, 1925

Hemingway, Ernest. "Soldier's Home" from <u>In Our Time</u>. New York: Charles Scribner's Sons, 1925

Hemingway, Ernest. <u>The Sun Also Rises</u>. New York: Charles Scribner's Sons, 1926.

Hemingway, Ernest. "A Clean Well Lighted Place" from <u>Winner Take Nothing</u>. New York: Charles Scribner's Sons, 1933.

Hemingway, Ernest. "Old Man at the Bridge" from <u>The Short Stories of Ernest Hemingway</u>. New York: Charles Scribner's

Sons, 1938.

Hemingway, Ernest. <u>For Whom The Bell Tolls</u>. New York: Charles Scribner's Sons, 1943.

Hemingway, Ernest. "Fifty Grand" from <u>The Hemingway Reader</u>, pp.393 – 417. New York: Charles Scribner's Sons, 1953.

Hemingway, Ernest. "Selected Letters" from <u>Ernest Hemingway On Writing.</u> Ed. Larry W. Phillips. New York: Touchstone, 1999.

Joyce, James. "Eveline" from <u>The Dubliners</u>. London: Grant Richards, 1914.

Mansfield, Katherine. <u>Bliss and Other Stories</u>. London: Constable and Company Limited, 1920

Miller, Arthur. <u>Death of a Salesman</u>. New York: Viking Press, 1949.

Orwell, George. <u>Animal Farm</u>. New York: Signet, 1946

Steinbeck, John. <u>Of Mice and Men</u>. New York: Triangle Books, 1937.

Thackeray, William Makepeace. <u>Vanity Fair</u>. London: Bradbury and Evans, 1848.

Twain, Mark. "A True Story, Repeated Word for Word As I Heard It." <u>The Atlantic Monthly</u> Nov. 1874: 591-4.

Williams, Tennessee. <u>A Streetcar Named Desire.</u> London: John Lehmann, 1949

Woolf, Virginia. <u>Mrs Dalloway.</u> New York: Harcourt, Brace and Company, 1925.

Biography of the Author

Glen Paul Hammond earned an Honours degree in Psychology, a Bachelor of Education and a Master of Arts in English Literature from the University of Toronto. He is a published author in the field of education, literature and history. He has been a therapist in Applied Behavioural Analysis and Verbal Modification Therapy. He now teaches English Literature at a private secondary school.

More books by the author are currently available:

THE RADLEYS OF KNOCKROUR

IONAD COINNE: MAC CARTHY'S BULL & O'CALLAGHAN'S COW

THOMAS FITZMAURICE & DESMOND, THE APE

TEN WAYS TO WIN AN ARGUMENT

For further reading see *SCRATCH* at http://scratch-the-irish-canadian.blogspot.ca/

Manufactured by Amazon.ca
Bolton, ON

33828653R00046